Francis Frith's
Piers

Photographic Memories

Francis Frith's
Piers

Tim Mickleburgh
Chairman of the National Piers Society

FRITH
BOOK Co

First published in the United Kingdom in 2000 by
Frith Book Company Ltd

British Library Cataloguing in Publication Data

Francis Frith's Piers
Tim Mickleburgh
ISBN 1-85937-237-6

Frith Book Company Ltd
Frith's Barn, Teffont,
Salisbury, Wiltshire SP3 5QP
Tel: +44 (0) 1722 716 376
Email: info@frithbook.co.uk
www.frithbook.co.uk

Printed and bound in Great Britain

Front Cover: St Annes, On the Pier 1906 53888

AS WITH ANY HISTORICAL DATABASE THE FRITH ARCHIVE IS CONSTANTLY BEING CORRECTED AND IMPROVED
AND THE PUBLISHERS WOULD WELCOME INFORMATION ON OMISSIONS OR INACCURACIES

Contents

Francis Frith: *Victorian Pioneer*

FRANCIS FRITH, Victorian founder of the world-famous photographic archive, was a complex and multi-talented man. A devout Quaker and a highly successful Victorian businessman, he was both philosophic by nature and pioneering in outlook.

By 1855 Francis Frith had already established a wholesale grocery business in Liverpool, and sold it for the astonishing sum of £200,000, which is the equivalent today of over £15,000,000. Now a multi-millionaire, he was able to indulge his passion for travel. As a child he had pored over travel books written by early explorers, and his fancy and imagination had been stirred by family holidays to the sublime mountain regions of Wales and Scotland. 'What a land of spirit-stirring and enriching scenes and places!' he had written. He was to return to these scenes of grandeur in later years to 'recapture the thousands of vivid and tender memories', but with a different purpose. Now in his thirties, and captivated by the new science of photography, Frith set out on a series of pioneering journeys to the Nile regions that occupied him from 1856 until 1860.

Intrigue and Adventure

He took with him on his travels a specially-designed wicker carriage that acted as both dark-room and sleeping chamber. These far-flung journeys were packed with intrigue and adventure. In his life story, written when he was sixty-three, Frith tells of being held captive by bandits, and of fighting 'an awful midnight battle to the very point of surrender with a deadly pack of hungry, wild dogs'. Sporting flowing Arab costume, Frith arrived at Akaba by camel seventy years before Lawrence, where he encountered 'desert princes and rival sheikhs, blazing with jewel-hilted swords'.

During these extraordinary adventures he was assiduously exploring the desert regions bordering the Nile and patiently recording the antiquities and peoples with his camera. He was the first photographer to venture beyond the sixth cataract. Africa was still the mysterious 'Dark Continent', and Stanley and Livingstone's historic meeting was a decade into the future. The conditions for picture taking confound belief. He laboured for hours in his wicker dark-room in the sweltering heat of the desert, while the volatile chemicals fizzed dangerously in their trays. Often he was forced to work in remote tombs and caves where conditions were cooler. Back in London he exhibited his photographs and was 'rapturously cheered' by members of the Royal Society. His reputation as a photographer was made overnight. An eminent modern historian has likened their impact on the population of the time to that on our own generation of the first photographs taken on the surface of the moon.

Venture of a Life-Time

Characteristically, Frith quickly spotted the opportunity to create a new business as a specialist publisher of photographs. He lived in an era of immense and sometimes violent change. For the poor in the early part of Victoria's reign work was a drudge and the hours long, and people had precious little free time to enjoy themselves. Most had no transport other than a cart or gig at their disposal, and had not travelled far beyond the

boundaries of their own town or village. However, by the 1870s, the railways had threaded their way across the country, and Bank Holidays and half-day Saturdays had been made obligatory by Act of Parliament. All of a sudden the ordinary working man and his family were able to enjoy days out and see a little more of the world.

With characteristic business acumen, Francis Frith foresaw that these new tourists would enjoy having souvenirs to commemorate their days out. In 1860 he married Mary Ann Rosling and set out with the intention of photographing every city, town and village in Britain. For the next thirty years he travelled the country by train and by pony and trap, producing fine photographs of seaside resorts and beauty spots that were keenly bought by millions of Victorians. These prints were painstakingly pasted into family albums and pored over during the dark nights of winter, rekindling precious memories of summer excursions.

The Rise of Frith & Co

Frith's studio was soon supplying retail shops all over the country. To meet the demand he gathered about him a small team of photographers, and published the work of independent artist-photographers of the calibre of Roger Fenton and Francis Bedford. In order to gain some understanding of the scale of Frith's business one only has to look at the catalogue issued by Frith & Co in 1886: it runs to some 670 pages, listing not only many thousands of views of the British Isles but also many photographs of most European countries, and China, Japan, the USA and

Canada – note the sample page shown above from the hand-written *Frith & Co* ledgers detailing pictures taken. By 1890 Frith had created the greatest specialist photographic publishing company in the world, with over 2,000 outlets – more than the combined number that Boots and W H Smith have today! The picture on the right shows the *Frith & Co* display board at Ingleton in the Yorkshire Dales. Beautifully constructed with mahogany frame and gilt inserts, it could display up to a dozen local scenes.

Postcard Bonanza

The ever-popular holiday postcard we know today took many years to develop. In 1870 the Post Office issued the first plain cards, with a pre-printed stamp on one face. In 1894 they allowed other publishers' cards to be sent through the mail with an attached adhesive halfpenny stamp. Demand grew rapidly, and in 1895 a new size of postcard was permitted called the court card, but there was little room for illustration. In 1899, a year after Frith's death, a new card measuring 5.5 x 3.5 inches became the standard format, but it was not until 1902 that the divided back came into being, with address and message on one face and a full-size illustration on the other. *Frith & Co* were in the vanguard of postcard development, and Frith's sons Eustace and Cyril continued their father's monumental task, expanding the number of views offered to the public and recording more and more places in Britain, as the coasts and countryside were opened up to mass travel.

Francis Frith died in 1898 at his villa in Cannes, his great project still growing. The archive he created continued in business for another seventy years. By 1970 it contained over a third of a million pictures of 7,000 cities, towns and villages. The massive photographic record Frith has left to us stands as a living monument to a special and very remarkable man.

Frith's Archive: *A Unique Legacy*

FRANCIS FRITH'S legacy to us today is of immense significance and value, for the magnificent archive of evocative photographs he created provides a unique record of change in 7,000 cities, towns and villages throughout Britain over a century and more. Frith and his fellow studio photographers revisited locations many times down the years to update their views, compiling for us an enthralling and colourful pageant of British life and character.

We tend to think of Frith's sepia views of Britain as nostalgic, for most of us use them to conjure up memories of places in our own lives with which we have family associations. It often makes us forget that to Francis Frith they were records of daily life as it was actually being lived in the cities, towns and villages of his day. The Victorian age was one of great and often bewildering change for ordinary people, and though the pictures evoke an impression of slower times, life was as busy and hectic as it is today.

We are fortunate that Frith was a photographer of the people, dedicated to recording the minutiae of everyday life. For it is this sheer wealth of visual data, the painstaking chronicle of changes in dress, transport, street layouts, buildings, housing, engineering and landscape that captivates us so much today. His remarkable images offer us a powerful link with the past and with the lives of our ancestors.

Today's Technology

Computers have now made it possible for Frith's many thousands of images to be accessed almost instantly. In the Frith archive today, each photograph is carefully 'digitised' then stored on a CD Rom. Frith archivists can locate a single photograph amongst thousands within seconds. Views can be catalogued and sorted under a variety of categories of place and content to the immediate benefit of researchers.

Inexpensive reference prints can be created for them at the touch of a mouse button, and a wide range of books and other printed materials assembled and published for a wider, more general readership - in the next twelve months over a hundred Frith local history titles will be published! The day-to-day workings of the archive are very different from how they were in Francis Frith's time: imagine the herculean task of sorting through eleven tons of glass negatives as Frith had to do to locate a particular

See Frith at www. frithbook.co.uk

sequence of pictures! Yet the archive still prides itself on maintaining the same high standards of excellence laid down by Francis Frith, including the painstaking cataloguing and indexing of every view.

It is curious to reflect on how the internet now allows researchers in America and elsewhere greater instant access to the archive than Frith himself ever enjoyed. Many thousands of individual views can be called up on screen within seconds on one of the Frith internet sites, enabling people living continents away to revisit the streets of their ancestral home town, or view places in Britain where they have enjoyed holidays. Many overseas researchers welcome the chance to view special theme selections, such as transport, sports, costume and ancient monuments.

We are certain that Francis Frith would have heartily approved of these modern developments in imaging techniques, for he himself was always working at the very limits of Victorian photographic technology.

The Value of the Archive Today

Because of the benefits brought by the computer, Frith's images are increasingly studied by social historians, by researchers into genealogy and ancestory, by architects, town planners, and by teachers and schoolchildren involved in local history projects.

In addition, the archive offers every one of us an opportunity to examine the places where we and our families have lived and worked down the years. Highly successful in Frith's own era, the archive is now, a century and more on, entering a new phase of popularity.

The Past in Tune with the Future

Historians consider the Francis Frith Collection to be of prime national importance. It is the only archive of its kind remaining in private ownership and has been valued at a million pounds. However, this figure is now rapidly increasing as digital technology enables more and more people around the world to enjoy its benefits.

Francis Frith's archive is now housed in an historic timber barn in the beautiful village of Teffont in Wiltshire. Its founder would not recognize the archive office as it is today. In place of the many thousands of dusty boxes containing glass plate negatives and an all-pervading odour of photographic chemicals, there are now ranks of computer screens. He would be amazed to watch his images travelling round the world at unimaginable speeds through network and internet lines.

The archive's future is both bright and exciting. Francis Frith, with his unshakeable belief in making photographs available to the greatest number of people, would undoubtedly approve of what is being done today with his lifetime's work. His photographs, depicting our shared past, are now bringing pleasure and enlightenment to millions around the world a century and more after his death.

Piers - *An Introduction*

THERE CAN BE very few people living in the United Kingdom who do not have fond memories of going to the seaside. As youngsters we love to play on the beach, whilst as adults, our first glimpse of the sea is often sufficient to bring back those childish urges. And what structure typifies a coastal resort more than a pier? How exciting it is to have the opportunity of walking out over the water without getting your feet wet!

The history of the seaside pier can be traced to the growth of towns like Scarborough and Margate in the late 1700s. It became the fashionable thing for the rich to go to the coast, where they could take the natural waters, as distinct from the waters at the mineral springs at inland spas - Bath is the prime example of such a spa. People strolled on jetties, which started to have extra functions as well as being merely for promenading.

Jetties, as early piers tended to be called, were also built for a more practical purpose - somewhere that boats could call. Inland transport was not anything to write home about; at this period, original Roman roads were still being used in many places. Thus it made sense for passengers to get to these new resorts by sea, and to land at a freshly-constructed jetty in the absence of an artificial or natural harbour.

Ryde Pier, built in 1813-4, was the earliest of the ninety or so seaside piers which were to be erected over the next hundred years. More famous, however, was Brighton Chain Pier, built in 1822-3 in the style of a suspension bridge. It attracted the patronage of King William IV, and appeared in paintings by both J M W Turner and John Constable. With facilities which included a camera obscura, shower baths, kiosks and shops, the pier certainly had a true pleasure function.

The pier craze soon started to gather momentum, and in the 1830s other English piers opened at Southend, Walton, Herne Bay, Southampton and Deal. Wales got its first pier in 1846 at Beaumaris, whilst even in Scotland a number of piers had been built before the end of the 1840s. These, though, tended to be more simple constructions, erected solely for ships to land.

Any resort of note felt that it needed a pier to enhance its status. During the peak decades for pier building in England and Wales, the 1860s and 1870s, an average of almost two structures opened each year. Eugenius Birch was the most renowned of a generation of pier engineers: he was responsible for designing no less than fourteen individual constructions. Brighton West was his undoubted masterpiece, and dates from 1866. There was a slight decline in the years that followed, but nevertheless piers opened at a rate of more than one every year right up until Burnham saw the light of day in 1911.

Not surprisingly, the British seaside was by then attracting a much wider clientele than just the wealthy. The increasingly powerful middle classes got into the habit of going to the seaside, as did the working classes once they were able to do so. A series of Factory Acts from 1833 onwards gradually reduced the length of the working week, while Parliament introduced four Bank Holidays under legislation of 1871. Hastings Pier opened on the first August Bank Holiday in 1872, with Cleethorpes Pier following suit a year later. In the industrial north, annual summer breaks became widespread. Whole towns would decamp en masse to the seaside - Skegness was known as 'Nottingham-by-the-Sea' owing to the influx of outside visitors.

Yet were it not for the expanded railway network, many seaside towns would have remained coastal backwaters. Track mileage grew from less than 2000 miles in 1840 to over 15,500 miles in 1870. Passengers were carried at speeds previously undreamed of: averages in excess of 40 mph were by no means uncommon. Again, the Government helped, passing a law in 1844 which compelled all companies to run at least one covered train - some early carriages were little more than cattle trucks - in each direction at no more than a penny a mile. The principle of travel for all was established.

It is perhaps worth noting that many pier promoters were connected with the railways. That was clearly true of Skegness, and also of Cleethorpes, where the pier soon came under the control of the Manchester, Sheffield and Lincolnshire Railway.

Why did pier building come to a conclusion? It was not due to the First World War, but largely because all places that wanted piers already had them. Indeed, some towns, such as Southsea and Great Yarmouth, boasted two. Blackpool, however, reigned supreme with three, and might have had a

further two. Yet even Blackpool must doff her cap to Atlantic City, New Jersey, where eight piers have existed over the years. This, incidentally, helps to demolish the myth that no piers were built overseas.

British purists, however, like to regard their piers as being somewhat superior to their American counterparts, which - so they say - lack the grace one associates with a traditional iron-built pier. Whether they are right or not, some of the last piers constructed in England were among the finest, and cost a lot of money. Weston-super-Mare's second pier, the Grand, involved expenditure of £120,000, and Brighton's Palace Pier cost even more at £137,000. Given price levels at the turn of the century, it is not surprising that this remained a record. For these vast sums, you certainly gained a substantial pier. Weston-super-Mare's Grand Pier had a vast pavilion, measuring 150ft by 90ft, which was capable of drawing crowds of two thousand to events ranging from opera to music hall. Brighton Palace Pier's pavilion contained a fifteen hundred-seater theatre, along with smoking and reading rooms.

Though new pier construction drew to a close (Weymouth Bandstand, which opened 1939, was the last of all), that did not prevent individual piers from continuing to develop in order to provide holidaymakers with the best possible entertainment. The inter-war period was arguably the 'golden age' for piers, with people wishing to put the horrors of conflict behind them. Clacton Pier was at the forefront of this amusement era when it erected its famous funfair. A dance hall, casino, swimming pool and children's theatre were among the new attractions provided. The late Lord Delfont (who was to become a major pier owner in the 1980s and 1990s through his company First Leisure) started his theatrical career as a dancer on this particular pier.

Elsewhere, new pavilions were erected at Southport, Penarth, Morecambe Central, Sandown, Colwyn Bay and Weston-super-Mare Grand amongst others. Shows and orchestral concerts were a popular feature of the successful pier - most of the famous names in music and show business were to perform on piers, from Sir Malcolm Sargent and Sir Henry Wood (of 'proms' fame) to Vera Lynn and David Nixon. And let us not forget George Formby, who played at St Annes. His name is associated with piers through the song 'The Wigan Boat Express', which is about the supposed mythical structure at Wigan. Piers, you see, are not meant to be found inland!

Ironically, however, there had been a pier of sorts at Wigan: Bankes Pier, a coal tippler on the Leeds and Liverpool Canal. Demolished in 1929, its stone base remained. Today, the entire site is covered by a tourist centre known as 'Wigan Pier' -Wigan appears to have had the last laugh after all! Yet the boats associated with piers in their heyday did not carry coal, but people. Thousands of

holiday-makers were brought to the piers by paddle steamers with evocative names like the 'Medway Queen' and 'La Marguerite'. Current trips by PS 'Waverley' help continue this long tradition.

So though economic depression affected certain areas, British piers gained from the affluence many others enjoyed. Those in employment had a shorter working week, paid holidays, and were gradually becoming car owners. Hence the boom years looked as if they could go on for ever. Alas, they did not.

The Second World War was to affect piers in various ways. Naval forces took over both Southend and Bognor Regis, along with Cowes Victoria on the Isle of Wight. Plymouth Hoe and Southsea Clarence were bomb casualties, whilst Minehead was pulled down to give guns a clear line of sight. This also caused the demolition of Deal's second pier, which had been already wrecked by a ship collision. Many piers were breached - that is, a section of decking was removed as a precaution against enemy invasion. However, I personally would have thought that a sophisticated enemy would have chosen to land at a secluded bay, miles away from a crowded built-up town like Great Yarmouth, Brighton or Bournemouth. Even if piers escaped sectioning, they remained closed and at the mercy of what the weather had to offer. Steamer services ceased, with pier railways running for the last time at Felixstowe and Herne Bay.

Running repairs, always essential for structures so vulnerable, took a back seat during war-time. Thus when the guns finally stopped firing in 1945, most piers needed a great deal of work to be done before they could open their gates to the public once again. Let us remember that these were still very much years of austerity, with rationing and shortages the order of the day. Given the economic environment, piers could be seen as an unnecessary luxury. So it was that some piers which survived the war did not last that long after it. Six piers disappeared from our coastlines in the 1950s, including Seaview Chain Pier, the first pier to be listed. At Cleethorpes they declined to re-attach the long pier neck; the iron was sold instead to help build a new stand for Leicester City Football Club. Along with Felixstowe, it was a shadow of its former self.

However, there were piers that thrived at that time: 5,750,000 people went on Southend Pier in the 1949-50 season, an all-time record. Deal got itself a new replacement pier, which was opened in 1957 by the Duke of Edinburgh. The new Southsea Clarence Pier followed 4 years later, a structure unique in being wider than its length. Changing leisure patterns, however, were hitting British resorts hard. No longer were iholiday-makers content with their week or fortnight at home; they were wanting to go overseas, where sunny weather was almost guaranteed. Cheap

package holidays on sale in Macmillan's 'You've never had it so good' Britain meant that they could afford to do this. Increased car ownership led trippers to move from town to town, affecting smaller resorts particularly. Obviously, piers suffered through a down-turn in visitor numbers - a further eight were demolished by 1980.

Yet by then the tide had started to turn. People were realising the architectural importance of seaside piers, and what would be lost if nothing were done. Groups were set up to try and save the structures at Southend, Clevedon and Brighton (West), supported by a National Piers Society. Bangor became the first preserved pier in 1988, followed by Clevedon and Swanage. The launch of the National Lottery helped the latter two, which both qualified for funding. Other piers also received money from this source.

Meanwhile, there remained the commercial successes, including the three piers at Blackpool. If piers adapted, their prime site meant they could thrive in a competitive leisure market. They were helped by the fight-back of Britain as a holiday destination, with visitors on short breaks and foreign tourists helping to maintain their viability. So though the 1990s saw Morecambe (Central), Shanklin and Ventnor pulled down, the outlook is by no means bleak. We can feel confident that piers can look forward to many years of history.

North-East England and East Anglia

Redcar
The Pier 1896 37594
The pier opened in 1873; it was constructed by Head Wrightson,
an engineering firm from nearby Stockton-on-Tees with a national
reputation. Pleasure cruises used to run from a small landing stage,
but a colliding ship wrecked this in 1885. Robert Conway's tariff list
is typical of late 19th-century advertising signs.

◄ **Redcar**
The Pier 1923 74245
The pier originally
measured 1300 feet, but
was a victim of
sectioning during the
Second World War. Mine
and storm damage
meant that the long neck
was removed, leaving
Redcar with a pier that
measured just 45 feet
beyond the pavilion.
Eventually this too was
demolished in 1980-81.

◄ **Redcar, The Pier 1913** 66393
There had been a 700-seater bandstand at the pierhead, which was burnt down during an 1898 fire. After a mobile bandstand on the promenade had proved inadequate for local entertainment needs, it was decided to construct a new pavilion, this time at the shore end. It opened in 1907, complete with a ballroom. The other entrance buildings remained the same.

▼ **Saltburn-by-the-Sea
The Pier Entrance
1913** 66354
This is the only pier remaining within Yorkshire's traditional boundaries. It was opened in 1869, and was to suffer over the years from a series of storms. These reduced its length from an initial 1500 feet. A cliff lift takes passengers to the pier's entrance.

◄ **Saltburn-by-the-Sea
The Pier 1932** 85275
In the 1970s, it seemed that Saltburn could lose its pier - the local authority actually applied for listed building consent to demolish it on safety grounds. But a public enquiry recommended that only the 13 end trestles should be removed. Today's 681ft-long pier has the same 1920s entrance building, which now contains amusements rather than a theatre.

Whitby, The New Pier 1913 66265A
Is this a true pier? It is left out of most reference books, but perhaps it should not be, for it is popular with promenaders, and provides a point of call for boats. It is complete with seats and lights, and only the pedant could completely ignore its claims.

Hull, The Pier 1903 49821
Known as either the Corporation or Victoria Pier, passenger ferries used to run from here to New Holland, where they connected with trains to Grimsby in the days before the Humber Bridge opened in 1981. Though the pontoon was removed, the pier still remains well-used by those wishing to sit and watch the boats go by.

Skegness
The Pier 1899 44350
East Coast piers had to go out a long way in order to
reach the sea at all tides. Skegness was certainly no
exception, and opened in 1881 with a length of 1817
feet. A small notice advertises R Connell,
one of the many divers who made a living
jumping off the end of piers.

Skegness, From the Pier 1910 62842
To encourage people to walk along a pier, attractions were invariably provided at the head. Those at Skegness included a 700-seater saloon cum concert hall, which was extended in 1898 with the addition of new refreshment rooms. Steamboat trips ran from a landing stage.

Skegness
The Pier Entrance c1955 S134078
Modernisation of the entrance took place in the late 1930s. The entrance then incorporated a café and shops either side of an archway. However, they were demolished to make way for a new large entrance building, containing amusement arcades. This opened in 1971.

Hunstanton, The Pier 1921 71033

Skegness, The Beach and the Pier c1955
S134150
A severe storm in January 1978 washed away two large sections of pier, leaving the theatre isolated at the seaward end. Rebuilding plans came to nothing, and the ruined pierhead and decking were eventually demolished. However, the section of pier passing over the central beach was extended in the 1990s.

**Hunstanton
The Pier 1901** 47646
Hunstanton Pier opened on Easter Sunday 1870 with a length of 830 feet. Paddle-steamers ran across the Wash to Skegness pier a year after the latter structure was built. A pavilion, described as being 'handsome and commodious' in a 1907 guide book, was added later.

**Hunstanton
The Pier 1921** 71033
The ironwork on this pier was particularly outstanding; structures like this help to show just why piers are regarded as important engineering constructions. At one stage, before the First World War, concerts were held in the pavilion every morning, afternoon and evening. This indicates the resort's popularity.

▼ Hunstanton, The Green and the Pier 1927 79723

Sad to say, a fire on 11 June 1939 destroyed the pavilion, which was never replaced. After 1945 the pier was used by roller-skaters, and it had a small zoo. The Ealing Comedy 'Barnacle Bill' (called 'All at Sea' for the American market) starring the late Sir Alec Guinness was filmed here in 1956.

▼ Hunstanton, The Pier c1950 H135072

A waxwork exhibition and bingo were among the many other post-war attractions here. This entrance building was replaced by a two-storey construction, which opened in 1964. It is sad that only this, together with one set of piles, now survives; the pier was badly storm-damaged in 1978.

▲ Cromer
The Pier 1902 49062

There had been earlier jetties here, but the seaside pier did not open until 1901. A pavilion was functional in 1905, after the extension of a seaward end bandstand. Lifeboats have been stationed here since 1923, and a new RNLI station was built in 1997-98. Traditional summer shows are still popular.

◄ **Felixstowe**
The Pier 1906 54640
Opened in 1906 with a length of half a mile, the pier incorporated an electric tramway - one of its cars is clearly visible in the photograph. Alas, the tram service ceased with the advent of war in 1939, while the pier's seaward section was demolished after the war was over. Today's pier measures just 450 feet. Can you spot the 'stuck on' elements in this photograph, such as the car and the groups of children in the foreground? This was a trick often used by photographers at the time to make their views more interesting. Even the steamer in the background is faked!

◄ **Great Yarmouth
The Britannia Pier 1904**

52337

The new Britannia Pier opened in 1901 with a temporary pavilion, which was pulled down to make way for a permanent pavilion a year later. It fell victim to fire in 1909, though it was replaced. This too was destroyed by a blaze in 1914, which was allegedly started by the Suffragettes, who had been refused permission to hold a meeting there. A third pavilion opened within months.

◀ Great Yarmouth
The Britannia Pier
1894 33385

This is a rare view of the first Britannia Pier, which opened in 1858. It was dogged by disasters, including a ship collision - something piers were often vulnerable to - and storm damage. The structure was finally pulled down in 1899, though work on a replacement began the following year.

▼ Great Yarmouth
The Britannia Pier
c1955 G56015

This view of the entrance shows just how much of the Britannia Pier is really land-based. Today the Pier Tavern and amusements are sited here, with a pavilion theatre - the fourth one on the site after another fire - further out to sea. Unlike the Wellington Pier, Britannia has always been privately owned.

◀ Great Yarmouth
The Wellington Pier
c1955 G56036

The first Wellington pier, built in 1853, was completely reconstructed after the council bought it. It re-opened in 1903, and included an impressive pavilion. The council also had the Winter Gardens transported from Torquay, and these became part of the pier complex, though they never went over the sea. Both the Winter Gardens and the Pier Theatre remain in use.

Lowestoft, The South Pier from the Sands 1896 37936
Like Great Yarmouth, Lowestoft has two piers. The older is the South Pier, built in 1846 as part of the harbour. A reading room was added in 1853–54, and a bandstand jetty in 1884. Both the bandstand and reading room were destroyed by fire in 1885, though a new reading room cum pavilion - that pictured - was constructed in 1889–91.

Lowestoft
The South Pier Reading Room 1896

37937

The reading room was badly damaged during the Second World War, and its remains were demolished. A new pavilion was opened by the Duke of Edinburgh in 1956. However, this was pulled down in the 1980s as part of an ultimately unsuccessful marina project. What with the adjacent Claremont Pier having had its decking closed, Lowestoft's piers have seen better days.

Clacton-on-Sea
The Bandstand and the Pier 1907 58934
Clacton's pier opened at the height of the pier boom in 1871; extensions in 1890-93 included a new polygonal head, complete with a pavilion. It was not until Ernest Kingsman bought the pier in 1922 that the series of inter-war amusement buildings associated with Clacton pier were added. The pier is much altered in recent years, but it is still amusement-dominated.

South-East England

Eastbourne, The Pier 1910 62958

Southend, The Pier 1898 41377
The longest seaside pier in the world, Southend's first pier lasted from 1830 to 1887. It was then replaced, and the new structure opened on 24 August 1890. Extensions were opened eight years later which took its length to a record-breaking 7080 feet. An electric railway took people to the pierhead.

▼ Southend, The Golden Hind and the Pier c1955 S155033

Southend Pier had become so popular that the rail track was doubled in 1929, and the Prince George steamer extension was built. During the Second World War it became HMS 'Leigh'. Afterwards a new electric train catered for millions of visitors, many from the East End of London, for whom Southend was their special resort.

▼ Southend, The Pier c1960 S155102

By 1960, visitor numbers had halved from the almost 6 million of the pier's post-war peak. Twenty years later, local councillors planned closure, but a last-minute rescue ensured its future. A new pier railway was opened in 1986 by Princess Anne. Southend was the favourite pier of Sir John Betjeman, first President of the National Piers Society.

▲ Margate
View on the Jetty 1887
19700

Though called the Jetty, this was a fully-fledged seaside pier, unlike the harbour wall that locals knew as the pier. Margate has long been a seaside resort, with claims that it had a landing jetty as far back as 1800. The structure illustrated was the first iron pier, which opened in 1855.

◀ **Margate**
The Jetty from the Fort
1897 39579
The jetty was also renowned for being the first to be designed by Eugenius Birch. Extensions were made in 1875-78, when the octagonal pierhead and pavilion were added. Further developments were made in 1893 and 1900. In 1897 the pier company recorded a profit of £1,689.

Margate
The Jetty 1918 68444
Like Brighton Chain
Pier, Margate Jetty once
had a camera obscura.
Alas, the jetty was
virtually destroyed by a
storm on 11 January
1978, after having
closed two years earlier
on safety grounds. Part
of the isolated pierhead
still survives as a
rusting tangle.

Pegwell, The Sea Front and the Pier c1880 12739
This little-known structure was built in 1878 for a local reclamation company, replacing an earlier jetty. Its main purpose was intended to be a landing stage for steamers, but few ever called. The company ended up going bankrupt, and the pier was pulled down inside a few years.

Deal, From the Pier Pavilion 1899 44203
This Kentish resort has had three piers over the years, although not concurrently. The first one, designed by Rennie, opened in 1838, but it decayed owing to storm damage and sandworm attack. It was washed away, and was replaced by a Birch-designed pier that opened in 1864. A pierhead pavilion followed in 1886.

Deal
The Bandstand and the Pier 1906 56911
Birch's pier was a victim of the Second World War:
only the tollhouses remained after the damaged
structure had been pulled down to assist the needs
of a coastal gun battery. However, it was replaced by
a reinforced concrete structure, built from 1954 to
1957. It remains council-controlled,
and popular with anglers.

**St Leonards
The Pier 1891** 29607
At least Hastings pier survives, unlike the pier which used to grace the coastline of its near neighbour. St Leonards pier lasted from 1891 to 1952, with its main feature the 600 to 700-seater pavilion pictured. This historic view shows the pier in the year that it opened, with its short-lived landing stage.

**Folkestone
The Pier 1895** 35530
The Victoria Pier
opened in 1888, and
included a 700-seater
pavilion. Famous names
that performed here
included Lily Langtry,
associated with the
future King Edward VII,
and the clog dancer
Dan Leno. This high
class variety proved
expensive, so new
leasees introduced less
costly entertainment
such as beauty contests
and film shows.

◄ **Dover**
Admiralty Pier 1901
48059
This was a traditional steamer pier; cross-channel ferries began operations in 1851, nine years before the railway's arrival. The pier was subsequently widened in the 1910s after Dover Marine station opened, initially just for military traffic. In 1994 the rail service ceased, though ships still go from here.

▲ **Dover, The Pier 1901** 48060
This pier was called the Promenade Pier to distinguish it from the Admiralty and Prince of Wales piers, which were both primarily used by steamers and trains. The Promenade Pier opened in 1893, and a pavilion was added six years later, but by 1925 it had become dilapidated. Repair costs were felt to be unjustifiable, and demolition followed in 1927.

▲ **Hastings**
The Pier 1890 22780
Another Birch pier, Hastings Pier opened in 1872, and included a seaward end pavilion capable of housing 2000 people. A landing stage was added in 1885. A notice outside one of the tollhouses, damaged by a storm in 1877 but repaired, shows that it would have cost you 2d to walk to the pierhead.

▲ **Folkestone, The Leas from the Pier 1901**
48054
During the First World War, the pier was popular with troops. However, it remained closed for the entire duration of the Second World War. On Whit Sunday 1943, a fire wrecked the pavilion; the rest of the pier was also badly damaged. Its ruins were demolished in 1954.

◀ **Hastings**
The Pier 1925 77984
Further development at the shoreward end included a rifle range and bowling alley. Known as the 'parade extension', this was sold to the council in 1913 to finance a new arcade, shops and a tea-room. The pavilion here is a 1922 replacement which was built after the original structure had been destroyed by fire. New owners took over in 2000.

**Eastbourne
The Pier 1910** 62958
Designed by Birch, the
pier opened in 1870. Its
first theatre seated 400,
and cost a mere £250 -
it eventually became a
cattle-shed at Lewes!
The saloons visible here
halfway along the
decking were added in
1901, the same year
that work on the new
pavilion was completed.

**Eastbourne
The Pier 1925** 77946
1925 marked the
building of a new 900-
seater music pavilion at
the shoreward end of
the pier. Already coach
traffic was having an
impact, bringing visitors
to sample the pier's
delights. We may be
thankful that although a
later entrance building
was wrecked by fire,
both the older theatre
and music pavilion can
still be seen today, and
the pier remains
successful.

Eastbourne
The Pier 1912 64968
Would an artist billed as 'The Gay Lord Quex'
perform today, I ask myself? It is hard to think that
in two years time many of the young men in this
photograph would be off to fight for King and
Country in the trenches of Europe. They deserved
to enjoy seaside life while they could.

Brighton, The Chain Pier 1870 B208003
This well-known early pier was engineered by Captain Samuel Brown, who had designed a smaller but similar structure, which opened at Leith near Edinburgh in 1821. The Chain Pier lasted from 1823 to 1896, falling victim to storms, neglect and a loss of business to the West Pier.

Brighton, The West Pier 1896 33717
Is this the finest pier of them all? It is certainly the only one deemed by the Department of the Environment to be worthy of Grade One listed status, which indicates its national importance. It opened in 1866, and the seaward end pavilion dates from 1893.

Brighton, The West Pier 1902 48497
Like many piers, there always seemed to be new developments taking place here. The southern pavilion was
rebuilt and extended only two years after its initial construction. Landing stages were built in 1896, and these were
also extended in 1901. The West Pier as we know it was slowly taking shape.

Brighton, From the West Pier 1921 71486
The penultimate stage of building was in 1916 - strangely enough, during the First World War - when a bandstand midway down the pier was removed as part of a widening process. A replacement Concert Hall followed. Only a new top-deck entrance remained to be added.

Brighton, The West Pier c1896 B2085009
Is this a foretaste of what was to come? Maybe not, but the West Pier has had a tough time of late. Listed building consent to demolish the seaward end was granted in the early 1970s, but this led to fierce local protests. A Trust now owns the pier, and has been given Lottery funding towards rebuilding.

Brighton, The Palace Pier 1902 48513
Though it opened in 1899, the 1800-seater theatre at the southern end was not completed until 1901, a full decade after work on the Palace Pier began. A pavilion and winter garden was added to the pier's centre in 1910. The theatre was dismantled in 1986, but was not replaced as had been planned.

Worthing, The Pier 1921 71444
There has only ever been the one pier at Worthing. The structure, built in 1862, is currently the seventh oldest surviving pier. Its first entertainments were provided by a 9-piece band, which performed here in 1874. The decking was widened in 1888-89, when a 650-seater pavilion was added at the pierhead.

Worthing
The Pier 1921 71445
Steamers used to call at the landing stage, but they were hampered by the low tides. Plans to double the pier's length to take more boat traffic were abandoned when it was realised that this would only make the water 6 inches deeper. Easter Monday 1913 saw the pavilion left isolated when the decking collapsed - London's Lord Mayor carried out the re-opening a year later.

Worthing, The Pier Head 1921 71457
Two kiosks had been added to the pier's entrance back in 1900, and these are shown here. The pier was taken over by Worthing Corporation in 1920, with a new shoreward end pavilion opening six years later. The pier's southern pavilion became a fire victim in 1933, but was replaced. A further amusement pavilion opened in 1937.

Worthing, On the Pier c1955 W147048
Troops were billeted at the shore-end pavilion during the Second World War, though it had re-opened to the general public by 1946. A facelift was carried out to this pavilion in 1958, with a £1.1 million renovation scheme taking place in 1979-82. Today the Pavilion Theatre houses dances and concerts, both of the classical and rock music variety.

Southern England

Bognor Regis
The Pier 1911 63786
The pier opened in 1865, with a seaward end pavilion constructed
in 1900. A new shoreward end complex was added a decade later,
including a cinema, arcade and theatre. Today the seaward end
pavilion is no more, a victim of storms in the 1960s. This
threatened pier, which was refused Lottery funding, hosts
an annual Birdman Rally.

▼ Southsea, The South Parade Pier c1950 S161007

The South Parade pier is the more traditional of Southsea's two piers. It was opened in 1879 by Princess Saxe-Weimar, and it was extensively rebuilt in the Edwardian era after a fire in 1904. A spacious pavilion included a 1200-seater theatre, which has since been replaced by a smaller structure. The rock opera 'Tommy' was filmed here.

▼ Cowes, The Victoria Pier 1908 60491

This is one of the shortest piers ever built at just 170 feet; it opened in 1902. A pavilion was constructed two years later. Regular ferries ran to both Southampton and Portsmouth, and the pier was used for the movement of troops during the First World War. The Royal Navy took it over for the Second World War.

▲ Cowes
The Victoria Pier 1923
74750

The Victoria Pier was a hub of waterfront activity, with sailing clubs making full use of its facilities, especially during Regatta week. Note the attached banner - advertising of this nature was very popular at the time. Ironically, this trend has not really been adopted in the more commercialised society of Britain as she is now.

◀ Cowes
The Old Pier c1955
C173011
Though called the Old Pier here, Cowes' other seaside pier - Cowes Royal - had long gone. In fact, it only lasted fifteen years, from 1867 to 1882. Sad to say, Cowes Victoria was to follow suit. No funds were available for repairs, hence the 'no admittance' notice half-hidden by a kiosk. The last of the structure was removed in 1965.

◀ **Ryde**
The Pier 1892 30033
The tramway closed in 1969, but the railway remained. Passengers can travel from the pierhead through to Shanklin, travelling on old electric stock that used to run the London Underground. A regular catamaran service goes to Portsmouth Harbour, with a café recently opened at the ferry terminal.

◄ Ryde
The Pier c1883 16297
This is the oldest true pier, opening in 1814. Eventually 2305 feet long, there were at one stage three strands of pier running alongside, incorporating a railway and tramway as well as the more traditional walkway. Shipping landed at the head, where there used to be a pavilion (demolished in 1971) and refreshment room.

▼ Sandown
From the Pier 1908

60556
It took a while for Sandown Pier to be erected: a Bill was passed by Parliament in 1864, but work did not begin until 1876. The pier finally opened three years later, measuring 360 feet. Extensions in 1895 took its length to 875 feet, with a pierhead pavilion among the new attractions.

◄ Sandown
The Pier 1935 86901
A landing stage opened the same year as the pierhead pavilion, catering for a generation of paddle steamers. Sandown Council took over the pier in 1918, and later amalgamated with their Shanklin neighbours. The new authority constructed a 1000-seater shoreward end pavilion, which opened in 1934.

▼ Sandown, The Pier c1951 S57020

Though the landing stage decayed during the Second World War, and the pier was breached for defence reasons, Sandown pier soon re-opened for business afterwards. Indeed, in the year of the Festival of Britain, it had its own 'Revels of 1951' to pull in the visitors.

▼ Sandown, The Pier c1955 S57022

The pierhead pavilion remained in use as a ballroom, before eventually becoming a victim of fire. Twinkle-toed holidaymakers were able to 'Dance to the Melotones'. The pier survived a £2 million blaze on August Bank Holiday Monday 1989, and is a commercial success. However, the theatre inside the redeveloped shoreward end pavilion ceased operating in 1997.

▲ Shanklin The Pier c1955 S104062

The Isle of Wight has been amongst the unluckiest areas for piers, with only four of its original structures now standing. Shanklin endured from 1890 to 1993; it would probably have been here today, had it not suffered severe damage from the hurricane which devastated southern England on 16 October 1987.

◄ **Totland Bay**
The Pier 1897 40385
The pier was overlooked by the Totland Bay Hotel. The same company used to own both the pier and the hotel, but the latter was demolished after Totland Bay was no longer able to attract the visitor numbers it recorded in the resort's heyday. The pier had been constructed in 1880 to replace an old wooden jetty.

◀ **Yarmouth
The Pier c1955** Y4002
Yarmouth Pier opened in
1876, and was built out
of wood, a common
material for the less
elaborate piers. Ferries
used to call, but from the
1930s they moved to a
nearby slipway - the ferry
to Lymington can be
seen in the photograph.
Excursions bring visitors
to this day, with the pier
benefiting from an
extensive rebuild in the
1980s and 1990s.

◄ Totland Bay
The Pier c1955 T65027
This was never the most entertainment-orientated of piers. A small amusement pavilion was built at the shoreward end, with a shelter at the head where boat passengers could wait. A post-Second World War Two rebuild saw the first steamer call for twenty years, the PS 'Lorna Doone'. The last major vessel to visit was MV 'Balmoral' in 1993.

▼ Netley
The Hospital from The Pier 1908 60464
This pier was built in 1856 to assist patients coming to the military Royal Victoria Hospital. It was used in both the Boer (1899-1902) and First World Wars (1914-18), and Netley became a popular place for convalescing soldiers and anglers. The pier was demolished in 1955.

◄ Southampton
The Royal Pier Pavilion 1908 60415
The name comes from the fact that the opening was carried out in 1833 by the Duchess of Kent and Princess, later Queen, Victoria. Its pavilion was added in 1894. Yet apart from the 1937 gatehouse, once a popular dance hall but currently closed, it is now hard to tell there was once a pier here, despite its being Britain's second oldest.

Hythe, The Pier Train c1955 H372025
This was always more of a landing pier; it opened in 1881 for use by the Hythe to Southampton ferry. Though Hythe Sailing Club used to have a clubhouse here, its main facility has long been the railway, which developed from a goods-only baggage line installed in 1909.

Hythe, The Ferry c1960 H372084
The 'Hotspur II' is seen here connecting with the train, currently operating a half-hourly service. Converted to take passenger traffic, it has used the same locomotives ever since the line opened in 1922. Extensive replanking of the pierhead was carried out in 1982, after development to the buildings there in 1970-71.

Boscombe, The Pier 1908 61191
The pier opened on 28 July 1889, three years after the Boscombe Pier Company had been formed. The local council took over the structure in 1904, at which time Southbourne pier (1888-1907) still existed, a pier they had declined to purchase. In 1905 the council erected both entrance and pierhead buildings.

Boscombe, The Pier 1931 84887
The pierhead was renewed in high alumna concrete in 1924-25 and 1927. The neck was similarly treated in 1958-60; this time it was rebuilt using a type of reinforced concrete that made wide use of non-ferrous components to help prevent marine corrosion.

Boscombe, The Pier c1955 B151013
The Mermaid Theatre, built at the head in 1961, was never used as a theatre, but was altered initially to provide a roller-skating rink. This theatre is now fenced off, whilst the pier neck stays open. The flat-roofed entrance that replaced the one shown has been critically described as an 'elongated bus shelter'.

**Bournemouth
The Pier from West Cliff 1897** 40553
The resort's first pier opened in 1861, replacing an
earlier wooden jetty. Badly storm-damaged, its
remains were pulled down. A temporary facility was
provided for the 1877 season, and the replacement
pier - designed by Birch - opened three years later.
Covered shelters and a bandstand were added
to the pierhead in 1885.

**Bournemouth
The Pier 1897** 40559
Further extensions were
made in 1894 and
1905; by this time the
pier's length had grown
to 1000 feet,
coincidentally the same
length as
Bournemouth's earlier
pier. The structure
contained a lengthy
landing stage, popular
with steamers travelling
along the South Coast.
10,000 people landed
here one 1901 Bank
Holiday weekend.

Bournemouth, The Pier Entrance 1900 45213
This attractive entrance building, which included a clock tower, no longer exists. At this part of the pier today is a two-storey octagonal leisure complex, incorporating shops, kiosks, show-bars and a multi-purpose hall. Costing £1.7 million, it opened in 1981. A new concrete pier neck dates from this time.

Bournemouth, The Beach and the Piers c1960 B163071
The pierhead had been reconstructed in 1950, and a concrete substructure was built ten years later to carry a new pier theatre. This explains why the pier looks bare. The structure in the foreground is actually Bournemouth Jetty, built in 1850, but pulled down in the 1970s.

Swanage
From the Pier 1897 40301
This is one of the more unusual piers: its
642ft-long neck does not go straight out to
sea, but veers rightward. It was built in 1895-
97, and was used widely by steamers.
However, boat traffic ended in 1966, when
the last paddler - the PS 'Embassy' - called.

Swanage, From the Pier 1897 40305
Views of this kind were very popular, as they enabled you to get a view of a town not available from elsewhere. The pier's turnstile can clearly be seen as part of the promenade, along with iron railings and a traditional pier lamp.

Swanage, The Pier 1897 40306
To the right of the pier we can see what was left of the structure the pier was built to replace. A few piles of the 1859 construction can still be seen: it was used as a diving platform until the 1950s. Swanage's newer pier was taken over by a Trust in 1994; it re-opened in 1998 thanks to Lottery funding.

South-West England and Wales

Weymouth
The Pier and Pavilion 1909 61589
This pier was known as the Commercial or Pleasure Pier, to
distinguish it from the town's old harbour pier. The pier pictured
here dates from 1840; a new passenger landing stage was built in
1888-89 for the Great Western Railway. A Pavilion Theatre was
constructed in 1908.

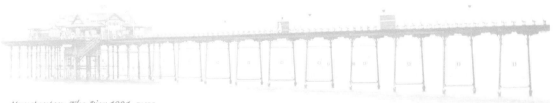

Hunstanton, The Pier 1921 71033

▼ **Weymouth, The Harbour and the Pier Pavilion 1913**   65656
The pier, seen here on the right, was burnt down in 1954. However, a second Pavilion Theatre opened in 1961, and is still fully functional today. The pier's prime purpose, though, is as a shipping terminal, with ferries going to both the Channel Islands and France.

▼ **Exmouth, The Pier 1896**   37624
The pier was built in 1865, and was originally used to unload materials needed for dock construction work. Yet it gained a pavilion in 1894 after being extended, which was sited to the right of what is visible on camera. In recent times, the pier has housed a car park.

▲ **Paignton
The Pier 1889**   21529
The purchasers of Teignmouth pier originally planned to have it moved and reconstructed at Paignton. However, structural difficulties prevented this, so the owner chose instead to build an entirely new pier at Paignton. This opened in 1879, and the pierhead was enlarged two years later.

◄ **Paignton
North Sands from the
Pier 1896** 38549
As a result of the 1881
developments, a billiard-
room was erected
connecting to the pavilion.
However, the pierhead was
burnt down by fire in 1919,
ushering in a period of
decline. Local authority
plans to buy the pier were
abandoned owing to
public opposition.

Paignton
The Sands and the Pier 1925 78476
Modernisation took place in 1980-81, costing a reported
£250,000. The shoreward end was widened, making the pier's
neck all the same width and new buildings were added. Further
development has occurred since the mid 1990s, under the
ownership of Mitchell Leisure, who also own Skegness pier.

Plymouth, The Pier 1889 22377
The Hoe Pier was the last to be designed by Eugenius Birch; he died a couple of months before it opened on 29 March 1884. It was just 480 feet long, with facilities which included shops, a clock tower and a landing stage.

Plymouth, The Pier 1902 48782
A pavilion was added in 1891, reputedly capable of seating 2000 people. The pier was struggling by the 1930s, though, with a loss of £1,276 recorded in 1934. Bomb damage in 1941 put an end to the controversy over ownership and the War Damage Commission paid the costs of its demolition in 1953.

◀ **Falmouth, The Prince of Wales Pier 1927**
80095
Reconstruction took place in 1951; the pier is currently owned by Carrick District Council. Both regular ferry services and excursions go from here, with different steps performing a similar function to railway station platforms. There are shops at the shoreward end, and shelters at the head.

Falmouth, The Prince of Wales Pier 1918

68777

The pier was named after the Prince of Wales (later King George V), who laid its foundation stone in 1903, two years prior to the pier's formal opening. It is the only pier in Cornwall, and even so there is disagreement over whether it is a proper seaside pier or not.

Ilfracombe The Pier 1899 43117

Demolition of the pier began in September 2000, amidst local objections. There had been a pier in the town since 1678; the most recent structure was largely rebuilt out of concrete in 1939-40 and 1952. It was a steamer pier, and unique in shape - its loss will be felt by residents.

Weston-Super-Mare The Grand Pier 1904

53003

'Pier now open', says one of the notices - 1904 was the year the general public could tread the boards of Weston's second pier. Another notice talks of special rates for railway passengers, indicating just how important trains were in bringing visitors to this and other resorts.

▼ **Weston-Super-Mare, The Grand Pier c1955** W69079
The pavilion had been destroyed by fire in 1930, but was replaced in 1932-33. This new construction was arguably the biggest single building put up on a pier in the inter-war years, though it never housed a theatre - it was home to a large fun fair instead. The pier's entrance was rebuilt in 1970.

▼ **Weston-Super-Mare, The View from the Birnbeck Pier 1887** 20330
The Old or Birnbeck Pier opened in 1867, and consisted of a span to a group of rocks called Birnbeck Island, and a North Jetty going on from there. A new pavilion and the Westward Jetty were added in 1898, with a lifeboat jetty following four years later.

▲ **Weston-Super-Mare
The Old Pier 1913**
65354A
The Westward Jetty (seen here on the left) lasted until 1923, when it was removed. Island amusements, including the water chute, fell victim to the Grand Pier's amusements in 1933. Today the pier has long been closed, though a land-based Pier View Information Bureau opened in 2000 - the first stage, let us hope, of a restoration programme.

◄ Clevedon, The Pier 1892

31251

This elegant pier was built using rails torn up from the South West Railway, and opened in 1867. It was hoped that paddle steamers would call on a main route from London to South Wales, but the pier had to rely on trips to places nearer home like Minehead, Ilfracombe and Chepstow.

◀ **Clevedon, The Pier and The Royal Pier Hotel c1965** C116048
Yet the pier survived a public enquiry in 1980, with the Environment Secretary calling it an 'exceptionally important building'. A Trust took the pier over, and rebuilding began in 1984. Final work was not completed until 1998, when Sir Charles Elton - great-great-grandson of the original pier company chairman - officiated at the opening ceremony.

◄ **Clevedon**
The Promenade
and the Pier 1913

65402

The wooden pierhead
was replaced by a cast
iron structure in 1892,
and an ornate pavilion
was added two years
later. Two spans collapsed
during routine testing in
1970, after the pier had
earlier been declared
unsafe. Its future seemed
very doubtful.

▼ **Penarth**
The Pier 1896 38723

When the pier opened in
1895, it was very plain,
with little in the way of
leisure facilities other
than the refreshment
room, florists and
weighing-machine seen
here. A large shoreward
end pavilion was not
added until 1927-28,
and a concrete landing
stage was built at the
same time.

◄ **Penarth**
From the Pier 1896

38464

A fire on August Bank
Holiday Monday 1931
destroyed a small
seaward end pavilion,
erected in 1907, along
with the mid-length
shelters and shops.
Steamer services ceased
in 1981, other than the
specials run by Waverley
Excursions. The pier
officially re-opened in
1998 after an extensive
restoration programme,
helped by Lottery
funding.

◄ **Mumbles
The Pier 1925** 77403
The main addition to the
pier itself has been the
landing jetty,
reconstructed in 1956.
However, the landward
end buildings, dating
from the same time,
were replaced in 1998
by a completely new
pavilion, engineered by
Masonwood
Architectural Consultants
who expanded the
original conception of
David Bateman. The
railway closed in 1960.

◀ Mumbles
The Pier 1898 40925

When it opened in 1898, the pier was the terminus for the Swansea and Mumbles Railway, whose trains can be seen taking people to their destination on the first official day of pier business. The pier had been promoted by a Mr John Jones Jenkins of the Rhonda and Swansea Bay Railway.

▼ Tenby
The Pier 1899 43346

This short pier, known as Tenby Royal Victoria, was built in 1897, and was extended two years later when it was officially opened by the Duke of York. Steamers used to call, while band concerts were given on the pierhead during the summer. The steel-arch pier had been totally demolished by 1953.

◀ Aberystwyth, The Pier Entrance 1925 77687

The pier was another Birch-designed affair, his only one in Wales. It opened in 1865, and gained itself a pavilion in 1896. The pavilion remains well used today, though there is no access to what remains of the neck, which has decayed over the years.

◀ **Bangor**
The Pier 1897 40044
This has always been an elegant and uncluttered pier, ever since it opened in 1896. It was going to be demolished, but thanks to the sterling work of Bangor City Council, the pier was restored, and re-opened in 1988. Kiosks sell refreshments and gifts, with the landing stage still capable of receiving vessels.

◄ **Beaumaris**
The Pier 1911 63924
Part piled and part
concrete, the pier first
opened in 1846, and
was then developed in
both 1872 and 1895.
There used to be a small
seaward end pavilion,
whereas there are now
just shelters here.
Today's pier is widely
used by anglers,
promenaders and those
on boat trips.

▼ **Llandudno**
The Pier c1877 8566
The pier opened to the
public in 1877; it
replaced a landing jetty
that had been pulled
down the previous year.
A seaward end
bandstand was erected
at this time, and a
shoreward end pavilion
was constructed seven
years after this.

◄ **Llandudno**
The Pier 1890 23250
The pier originally
measured an impressive
1234 feet, but this was
extended to 2295 feet
when an extension
opened in 1884 that
took the pier past where
the Grand Hotel is today,
right to the main
promenade. A new
landing stage was added
in 1891, and was
reinforced in 1904.

Llandudno, The Pier 1908 60755
The diversion from the present side entrance at Marine Drive can clearly be seen here. In 1905 a pavilion was built on the pierhead; two years later the pier was damaged by a colliding ship. Major alterations were made to both the pier and landing stage in 1938.

Llandudno, The Pier Entrance c1955 L71378
The shoreward end pavilion, empty since 1990, was damaged by fire in 1994, and was later demolished. However, there is still live entertainment in the hotel bar, even if this is a sad come-down from the days when the pier was supposed to have the best seaside orchestra in the country. Nevertheless, Llandudno remains a popular pier.

Colwyn Bay
The Pier 1900 46266
The pier's current owners, Anne and Mike Paxman, live on the pier, and have done much since taking it over in 1994 to keep the pier in business. Originally opened in 1900, it contained a 2500-seater pavilion. The present closed pavilion only dates from 1934; its art-deco style is impressive.

North-West England, Scotland and Northern Ireland

Extract from: **New Brighton, The Pier 1900** 45165

New Brighton, The Pier 1900 45165
There were once ten piers on the River Mersey,
though only New Brighton was ever regarded as
being a seaside pier. It opened in 1867, and
included a handsome saloon, refreshment rooms,
shelters, a pier orchestra and a tower from where
one could watch the ships go by.

▼ **New Brighton, The 'Royal Iris' Approaching the Pier c1960** N14021
After being bought by Wallasey Corporation in 1928, the pier gained a new pavilion
- this was deemed to be cheaper than carrying out repairs to the existing structure.
Sad to say, ferry services eventually ceased, causing visitor numbers to drop. The
pier closed in 1972, and was pulled down five years later.

▼ **Southport, The Pier 1891** 28558
Opened back in 1860, this is now the oldest surviving iron pier. Extensions some
eight years later took its length to 4380 feet, second only to Southend. Though
currently shorter (3633 feet), the pier still holds the 'runner up' slot. A tramway
took passengers to catch the steamers, which landed at the pierhead.

▲ **Southport
The Pier c1955** S160114
Over the years, much
land has been reclaimed,
with the present-day pier
having to go over a lake,
a miniature-golf course
and a road before
reaching the sea. The
pavilion pictured here
was destroyed by fire in
1957. Restoration work,
supported by the National
Lottery, is scheduled for
completion in 2001.

◄ **St Annes**
On the Pier 1906 53888
At one stage, there were piers at both St Annes and its close neighbour, Lytham. The latter's pier, however, was pulled down in 1960. St Annes pier opened in 1885, with extensions following in 1904. These included a new pierhead entrance, and a handsome Moorish pavilion which held 1000 people.

St Annes, The Pier Pavilion 1906 53890
The Moorish pavilion was joined by a Floral Hall in 1910, which also became a venue for concerts. Alas, both structures are no more. A fire destroyed the pavilion in 1974, with another blaze wrecking the Floral Hall eight years later. Refurbishment of the rest of the pier occurred in the early 1990s.

Blackpool, The Victoria Pier 1894 33951
This, the newest of the three Blackpool piers, opened in 1893, complete with a Grand Pavilion. In 1930 it changed its name to Blackpool South Pier. The pavilion was hit by fire in 1954, 1958 and 1964, being ultimately replaced by a new structure, which took just 12 weeks to build. This itself was demolished in 1998.

**Blackpool
The South Pier
from the Wellington Hotel 1890** 22881
The pier opened in 1868 as the South Pier, then
changed its name to Blackpool Central when the
Victoria (now South) Pier opened. Over the years it
became known as the 'People's Pier', specialising in
a vast range of amusement activities. A more genteel
pier would not have been so covered
in advertisements!

Blackpool
From the South Pier 1890 22868
At the end of the main Central (nee South) Pier
was a 400ft-long low-water jetty, clearly visible
here. This lasted right up until the 1970s. The
first major work on the pier involved altering
the entrance building in 1877. Further
development took place in 1903.

Blackpool
The South Pier 1890 22875
We cannot see this view of the Central (South) pier today, thanks
to the construction of the later Victoria (South) pier. But whatever
the reason, Blackpool has somehow managed to avoid the sharp
decline in trade since the Second World War that other resorts
have seen. New developments, such as a Big Wheel added in
1990, have helped to maintain business.

Blackpool
The Central Pier 1906 53855

The shoreward end White Pavilion was added during the 1903 entrance work, and later housed dancing. It was demolished in 1966. Facilities on the pier during the Edwardian age included an electric grotto railway, and a shop where glass could be engraved.

St Annes, The Pier Pavilion 1906 53890

Blackpool, The North Pier 1890 22880
The oldest and architecturally the finest of Blackpool's piers, the North Pier opened in 1863 to the designs of Eugenius Birch. An Indian Pavilion and bandstand were added to the pierhead in the 1870s. A new pier tramway was installed in 1990, though the landing and fishing jetty - lately used as a helicopter landing pad - suffered severe storm damage in 1997.

Fleetwood, The Pier 1918 68413
Always in the shadow of Blackpool and its three piers, Fleetwood pier was not built until 1910, and a pavilion was added the following year. A fire destroyed much of the pier's buildings on 25 August 1952, and the rebuilding of the 'New Super Pier' began a year later.

▼ Morecambe, The West End Pier 1896 37387

Seen here in the year of its opening, 1896, Morecambe Pier's most impressive feature was a large pavilion. The pier was extended in 1898, but storms in 1907 and 1927 halved the pier's length to 900 feet. In 1917 the pavilion, which had hosted the Viennese Orchestra, was destroyed by fire.

▼ Morecambe, The West End Pier 1899 42867

After the Second World War, people flocked to the West End Pier to take part in open-air dancing. Indeed, that was one reason why many people are said to have retired here. However, in 1977 a severe storm left sections of the pier isolated. Rather than pay the £500,000 quoted for repairs, the pier was pulled down the next year.

▲ Morecambe The Central Pier 1888

21080

The Central Pier was the older of the two: it opened in 1869 and was enlarged during the following decade. A large pierhead was ideal for the steamers, which used to call in the days before the First World War. Weekly tickets costing 1s (5p) were available for regular visitors.

◀ **Morecambe
The Central Pier 1906**

56106

By the turn of the century a pavilion was added, which was subsequently replaced in 1935-36. In 1986, however, the pier closed after the seaward end decking gave way during a disco. Fire later damaged the landward end amusement arcade. Though repair work began in 1990, the pier was eventually pulled down, leaving Morecambe with just an historic stone jetty.

▼ Coniston, The Gondola Pier 1906 54243

Originally called Pier Cottage, Coniston Pier was later joined by structures at Lake Bank and Monk Coniston. These were eventually removed, though the National Trust added piers at Park-a-Moor and Brantwood in the 1980s. Coniston Pier, in reality a mere landing stage, is known as the Gondola Pier after a steam yacht first launched on the lake in 1859.

▼ Bowness, The Pier c1955 B166019

The main piers on England's longest lake are at Ambleside, Lakeside and Bowness. These were built at the time of the coming of the railway in 1869, when a ferry service - now operated by Windermere Land Cruises - began that same year. At Bowness there are two other landing stages called Pier One and Pier Two.

▲ Ramsey, The Beach and the Pier 1893
33061
The pier was built in 1886 for the Isle of Man Harbour Board, and remains publicly-owned. It eventually incorporated a 3-foot gauge tramway, which connected with steamers that landed at the pierhead. Prior to the First World War, 36,000 people annually arrived at Ramsey that way.

◄ **Ramsey**
The Pier 1895 36746
In 1969, just 3,054 passengers disembarked, and ferry services ended after the 1970 season. The tramway ran for the last time in 1981, with vandalism causing the entire pier to shut down a decade later. Money continues to be spent on upkeep, and the pier opens on special occasions.

◄ **Aberdour, The Stone Pier 1900** 45912
In addition to the old stone pier, there was a more modern construction, seen here on the right. The east coast of Scotland has fewer piers than the west coast, largely because artificial harbours had already been built before the pier building age. Both of the piers seen here served as landing places.

◀ **Wigan**
The Pier c1960 W98011
This is not the joke that many think, but a landing stage for coal traffic. Demolition loomed in the 1970s, but then the derelict wharfside was turned into a museum complex that won the British Tourist Authority's 'Come to Britain' trophy for 1985. The pier joined in 1996's 'Year of the Pier' celebrations.

▼ **Ayr, The Pier 1900** 45999
Like many Scottish piers, the one at Ayr formed part of the harbour. Ironically, sailings from Glasgow were better patronised before the coming of the railway! Ayr remained an important port for packet boats from 1840 until the outbreak of the Second World War. Cruises recommenced in 1975, with PS 'Waverley' based here during her main season.

◀ **Dunoon**
The Pier 1901 47423
Since the demolition of Portobello pier in 1917, this is probably the finest Scottish pier. There has been a structure on the site ever since 1835; the present pier was opened in 1898 by Lord and Lady Malcolm. All the buildings have a distinct Tudor look, and were renovated in 1980-81 at a cost of £175,000.

Kirn, Leaving the Pier c1955 K52066
This is one of the older Scottish piers, dating from 1845. But with a change in traffic flow, only four calls a day for the Gourock-Dunoon car ferry were made by the time this photo was taken, along with certain excursion trips. The final visitor was the 'Cowal' in December 1963.

**◀ Dunoon
The Pier 1904** 52620
Though popular with promenaders, this has always been a shipping pier, able to handle two vessels at once if need be. During the Second World War, operations were limited to daylight hours. Continued improvements and repiling still took place then, unlike at its counterparts south of the border.

**▼ Loch Katrine
The Trossachs Pier
c1890** L93002
Some Scottish lochs reach to the sea, whilst others are purely inland, with piers around their edges. Loch Katrine is one of the latter, served by boats that largely cater for tourists today. Near to the pier is a visitors' centre, only open during the season, and a tearoom.

◀ Oban, The Railway Station and the New Pier c1900 04001
Oban actually boasts four piers, one more than Blackpool! Two, however, the South and the Lighthouse piers, are purely industrial structures. The railway pier was built in 1880, and is the headquarters for the Hebridean operations of the shipping company CalMac. To its north can be seen - appropriately enough - Oban North Pier, ten years older and once a steamer pier.

Bangor, The Esplanade 1897 40241
The North Pier at Bangor was used by steamers going to Belfast; it had flagpoles, wrought iron seats and gas lamps. Daily sailings ran until 1916, though excursions continued after that date. Some services to Stranraer were diverted to start from here instead of Larne in the 1930s. The pier was demolished in 1980, when it was described as 'an impressive feat of engineering' by a local paper.

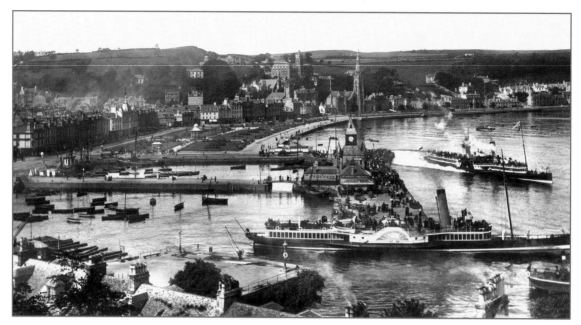

Rothesay, The Pier 1897 39836
Rothesay was the place where trippers from Glasgow came; its esplanade was built in 1870 to cater for those making the legendary pilgrimage 'doon the watter'. The town had a harbour as early as 1752, and a separate pier was finally added in the 1860s. New pier buildings were constructed in 1885, and extensions were completed fourteen years later.

Rothesay, From the Promenade c1955 R61011
The resort started to decline before 1914, though it remained popular right up until 1939. It has since been unable to regain its former glory - the clock tower seen here was destroyed by fire. Yet boats still call in considerable numbers, whilst the 1899 Victorian toilets gained listed status and were restored in the 1990s.

Index

Frith Book Co Titles

www.frithbook.co.uk

The Frith Book Company publishes over 100 new titles each year. A selection of those currently available are listed below. For latest catalogue please contact Frith Book Co.

Town Books 96pp, 100 photos. County and Themed Books 128pp, 150 photos (unless specified). All titles hardback laminated case and jacket except those indicated pb (paperback)

Around Bakewell	1-85937-113-2	£12.99	Exmoor	1-85937-132-9	£14.99
Around Barnstaple	1-85937-084-5	£12.99	Around Falmouth	1-85937-066-7	£12.99
Around Bath	1-85937-097-7	£12.99	Glasgow (pb)	1-85937-190-6	£9.99
Berkshire (pb)	1-85937-191-4	£9.99	Around Great Yarmouth	1-85937-085-3	£12.99
Around Blackpool	1-85937-049-7	£12.99	Around Guildford	1-85937-117-5	£12.99
Around Bognor Regis	1-85937-055-1	£12.99	Hampshire	1-85937-064-0	£14.99
Around Bournemouth	1-85937-067-5	£12.99	Around Harrogate	1-85937-112-4	£12.99
Brighton (pb)	1-85937-192-2	£8.99	Hertfordshire (pb)	1-85937-247-3	£9.99
British Life A Century Ago	1-85937-103-5	£17.99	Around Horsham	1-85937-127-2	£12.99
Buckinghamshire (pb)	1-85937-200-7	£9.99	Around Ipswich	1-85937-133-7	£12.99
Around Cambridge	1-85937-092-6	£12.99	Ireland (pb)	1-85937-181-7	£9.99
Cambridgeshire	1-85937-086-1	£14.99	Isle of Man	1-85937-065-9	£14.99
Canals and Waterways	1-85937-129-9	£17.99	Isle of Wight	1-85937-114-0	£14.99
Cheshire	1-85937-045-4	£14.99	Kent (pb)	1-85937-189-2	£9.99
Around Chester	1-85937-090-x	£12.99	Around Leicester	1-85937-073-x	£12.99
Around Chichester	1-85937-089-6	£12.99	Leicestershire (pb)	1-85937-185-x	£9.99
Churches of Berkshire	1-85937-170-1	£17.99	Around Lincoln	1-85937-111-6	£12.99
Churches of Dorset	1-85937-172-8	£17.99	Lincolnshire	1-85937-135-3	£14.99
Colchester (pb)	1-85937-188-4	£8.99	London (pb)	1-85937-183-3	£9.99
Cornwall	1-85937-054-3	£14.99	Around Maidstone	1-85937-056-x	£12.99
Croydon Living Memories (pb)			New Forest	1-85937-128-0	£14.99
	1-85937-162-0	£9.99	Around Newark	1-85937-105-1	£12.99
Cumbria	1-85937-101-9	£14.99	Around Newquay	1-85937-140-x	£12.99
Dartmoor	1-85937-145-0	£14.99	North Devon Coast	1-85937-146-9	£14.99
Around Derby	1-85937-046-2	£12.99	North London	1-85937-206-6	£14.99
Derbyshire (pb)	1-85937-196-5	£9.99	Northumberland and Tyne & Wear		
Devon	1-85937-052-7	£14.99		1-85937-072-1	£14.99
Dorset	1-85937-075-6	£14.99	Norwich (pb)	1-85937-194-9	£8.99
Dorset Coast	1-85937-062-4	£14.99	Around Nottingham	1-85937-060-8	£12.99
Down the Severn	1-85937-118-3	£14.99	Nottinghamshire (pb)	1-85937-187-6	£9.99
Down the Thames	1-85937-121-3	£14.99	Around Oxford	1-85937-096-9	£12.99
Around Dublin	1-85937-058-6	£12.99	Oxfordshire	1-85937-076-4	£14.99
East Sussex	1-85937-130-2	£14.99	Peak District	1-85937-100-0	£14.99
Around Eastbourne	1-85937-061-6	£12.99	Around Penzance	1-85937-069-1	£12.99
Edinburgh (pb)	1-85937-193-0	£8.99	Around Plymouth	1-85937-119-1	£12.99
English Castles	1-85937-078-0	£14.99	Around St Ives	1-85937-068-3	£12.99
Essex	1-85937-082-9	£14.99	Around Scarborough	1-85937-104-3	£12.99
Around Exeter	1-85937-126-4	£12.99	Scotland (pb)	1-85937-182-5	£9.99

Available from your local bookshop or from the publisher

Frith Book Co Titles (continued)

Scottish Castles	1-85937-077-2	£14.99		Around Torbay	1-85937-063-2	£12.99
Around Sevenoaks and Tonbridge	1-85937-057-8	£12.99		Around Truro	1-85937-147-7	£12.99
Around Southampton	1-85937-088-8	£12.99		Victorian & Edwardian Kent	1-85937-149-3	£14.99
Around Southport	1-85937-106-x	£12.99		Victorian & Edwardian Maritime Album		
Around Shrewsbury	1-85937-110-8	£12.99			1-85937-144-2	£17.99
Shropshire	1-85937-083-7	£14.99		Victorian & Edwardian Yorkshire	1-85937-154-x	£14.99
South Devon Coast	1-85937-107-8	£14.99		Victorian Seaside	1-85937-159-0	£17.99
South Devon Living Memories	1-85937-168-x	£14.99		Warwickshire (pb)	1-85937-203-1	£9.99
Staffordshire (96pp)	1-85937-047-0	£12.99		Welsh Castles	1-85937-120-5	£14.99
Stone Circles & Ancient Monuments				West Midlands	1-85937-109-4	£14.99
	1-85937-143-4	£17.99		West Sussex	1-85937-148-5	£14.99
Around Stratford upon Avon	1-85937-098-5	£12.99		Wiltshire	1-85937-053-5	£14.99
Sussex (pb)	1-85937-184-1	£9.99		Around Winchester	1-85937-139-6	£12.99

Frith Book Co titles available Autumn 2000

Cotswolds (pb)	1-85937-230-9	£9.99	Sep		English Country Houses	1-85937-161-2	£17.99	Oct
Cornish Coast	1-85937-163-9	£14.99	Sep		Folkestone (pb)	1-85937-124-8	£9.99	Oct
County Durham	1-85937-123-x	£14.99	Sep		Humberside	1-85937-215-5	£14.99	Oct
Dorset Living Memories	1-85937-210-4	£14.99	Sep		Manchester (pb)	1-85937-198-1	£9.99	Oct
Dublin (pb)	1-85937-231-7	£9.99	Sep		Norfolk Living Memories	1-85937-217-1	£14.99	Oct
Herefordshire	1-85937-174-4	£14.99	Sep		Preston (pb)	1-85937-212-0	£9.99	Oct
Kent Living Memories	1-85937-125-6	£14.99	Sep		Reading (pb)	1-85937-238-4	£9.99	Oct
Leeds (pb)	1-85937-202-3	£9.99	Sep		Salisbury (pb)	1-85937-239-2	£9.99	Oct
Ludlow (pb)	1-85937-176-0	£9.99	Sep		South Hams	1-85937-220-1	£14.99	Oct
Norfolk (pb)	1-85937-195-7	£9.99	Sep		Suffolk (pb)	1-85937-221-x	£9.99	Oct
North Yorks (pb)	1-85937-236-8	£9.99	Sep		Swansea (pb)	1-85937-167-1	£9.99	Oct
Somerset	1-85937-153-1	£14.99	Sep		West Yorkshire (pb)	1-85937-201-5	£9.99	Oct
Surrey (pb)	1-85937-240-6	£9.99	Sep					
Tees Valley & Cleveland	1-85937-211-2	£14.99	Sep		Around Aylesbury (pb)	1-85937-227-9	£9.99	Nov
Thanet (pb)	1-85937-116-7	£9.99	Sep		Around Bradford (pb)	1-85937-204-x	£9.99	Nov
Tiverton (pb)	1-85937-178-7	£9.99	Sep		Around Chichester (pb)	1-85937-228-7	£9.99	Nov
Victorian and Edwardian Sussex					East Anglia (pb)	1-85937-265-1	£9.99	Nov
	1-85937-157-4	£14.99	Sep		East London	1-85937-080-2	£14.99	Nov
Weymouth (pb)	1-85937-209-0	£9.99	Sep		Gloucestershire	1-85937-102-7	£14.99	Nov
Worcestershire	1-85937-152-3	£14.99	Sep		Greater Manchester (pb)	1-85937-266-x	£9.99	Nov
Yorkshire Living Memories	1-85937-166-3	£14.99	Sep		Hastings & Bexhill (pb)	1-85937-131-0	£9.99	Nov
					Helston (pb)	1-85937-214-7	£9.99	Nov
British Life A Century Ago (pb)					Lancaster, Morecombe & Heysham (pb)			
	1-85937-213-9	£9.99	Oct			1-85937-233-3	£9.99	Nov
Camberley (pb)	1-85937-222-8	£9.99	Oct		Peterborough (pb)	1-85937-219-8	£9.99	Nov
Cardiff (pb)	1-85937-093-4	£9.99	Oct		Piers	1-85937-237-6	£17.99	Nov
Carmarthenshire	1-85937-216-3	£14.99	Oct		Wiltshire Living Memories	1-85937-245-7	£14.99	Nov
Cheltenham (pb)	1-85937-095-0	£9.99	Oct		Windmills & Watermills	1-85937-242-2	£17.99	Nov
Cornwall (pb)	1-85937-229-5	£9.99	Oct		York (pb)	1-85937-199-x	£9.99	Nov

See Frith books on the internet www.frithbook.co.uk

FRITH PRODUCTS & SERVICES

Francis Frith would doubtless be pleased to know that the pioneering publishing venture he started in 1860 still continues today. A hundred and forty years later, The Francis Frith Collection continues in the same innovative tradition and is now one of the foremost publishers of vintage photographs in the world. Some of the current activities include:

Interior Decoration

Today Frith's photographs can be seen framed and as giant wall murals in thousands of pubs, restaurants, hotels, banks, retail stores and other public buildings throughout the country. In every case they enhance the unique local atmosphere of the places they depict and provide reminders of gentler days in an increasingly busy and frenetic world.

Product Promotions

Frith products are used by many major companies to promote the sales of their own products or to reinforce their own history and heritage. Frith promotions have been used by Hovis bread, Courage beers, Scots Porage Oats, Colman's mustard, Cadbury's foods, Mellow Birds coffee, Dunhill pipe tobacco, Guinness, and Bulmer's Cider.

Genealogy and Family History

As the interest in family history and roots grows world-wide, more and more people are turning to Frith's photographs of Great Britain for images of the towns, villages and streets where their ancestors lived; and, of course, photographs of the churches and chapels where their ancestors were christened, married and buried are an essential part of every genealogy tree and family album.

Frith Products

All Frith photographs are available Framed or just as Mounted Prints and Posters (size 23 x 16 inches). These may be ordered from the address below. From time to time other products - Address Books, Calendars, Table Mats, etc - are available.

The Internet

Already twenty thousand Frith photographs can be viewed and purchased on the internet. By the end of the year 2000 some 60,000 Frith photographs will be available on the internet. The number of sites is constantly expanding, each focussing on different products and services from the Collection.
The main Frith sites are listed below.
www.francisfrith.co.uk
www.frithbook.co.uk

See the complete list of Frith Books at:
www.frithbook.co.uk
This web site is regularly updated with the latest list of publications from the Frith Book Company. If you wish to buy books relating to another part of the country that your local bookshop does not stock, you may purchase on-line.

For further information, trade, or author enquiries please contact us at the address below:
The Francis Frith Collection, Frith's Barn, Teffont, Salisbury, Wiltshire, England SP3 5QP.
Tel: +44 (0)1722 716 376 Fax: +44 (0)1722 716 881 Email: uksales@francisfrith.com

See Frith books on the internet www.frithbook.co.uk

TO RECEIVE YOUR FREE MOUNTED PRINT

Mounted Print
Overall size 14 x 11 inches

Cut out this Voucher and return it with your remittance for £1.50 to cover postage and handling, to UK addresses. For overseas addresses please include £4.00 post and handling. Choose any photograph included in this book. Your SEPIA print will be A4 in size, and mounted in a cream mount with burgundy rule lines, overall size 14 x 11 inches.

Order additional Mounted Prints at HALF PRICE (only £7.49 each*)

If there are further pictures you would like to order, possibly as gifts for friends and family, purchase them at half price (no additional postage and handling required).

Have your Mounted Prints framed*

For an additional £14.95 per print you can have your chosen Mounted Print framed in an elegant polished wood and gilt moulding, overall size 16 x 13 inches (no additional postage and handling required).

---

* IMPORTANT!
These special prices are only available if ordered using the original voucher on this page (no copies permitted) and at the same time as your free Mounted Print, for delivery to the same address

---

Frith Collectors' Guild

From time to time we publish a magazine of news and stories about Frith photographs and further special offers of Frith products. If you would like 12 months FREE membership, please return this form.

Send completed forms to:
The Francis Frith Collection, Frith's Barn, Teffont, Salisbury, Wiltshire SP3 5QP

Voucher for **FREE** and Reduced Price Frith Prints

Picture no.	Page number	Qty	Mounted @ £7.49	Framed + £14.95	Total Cost
		1	**Free of charge***	£	£
			£7.49	£	£
			£7.49	£	£
			£7.49	£	£
			£7.49	£	£
			£7.49	£	£

Please allow 28 days for delivery *** Post & handling**	**£1.50**
Book Title . . . . **Total Order Cost**	**£**

Please do not photocopy this voucher. Only the original is valid, so please cut it out and return it to us.

I enclose a cheque / postal order for £ . . . .
made payable to 'The Francis Frith Collection'
OR please debit my Mastercard / Visa / Switch / Amex card
(credit cards please on all overseas orders)

Number . . . .

Issue No(Switch only) . . . . .Valid from (Amex/Switch) . . . .

Expires . . . . Signature . . . .

Name Mr/Mrs/Ms . . . .

Address . . . .

. . . .

. . . . Postcode . . . .

Daytime Tel No . . . .   Valid to 31/12/02

The Francis Frith Collectors' Guild
Please enrol me as a member for 12 months free of charge.

Name Mr/Mrs/Ms . . . .

Address . . . .

. . . .

. . . . Postcode . . . .

Free Print - see overleaf